NOT JUST ANOTHER BIGFOOT ENCOUNTER

NOT JUST ANOTHER BIGFOOT ENCOUNTER

THEY CAME OUT OF THE SHADOWS...

CURTIS JONES

Curtis Jones
Not Just Another Bigfoot Encounter

All rights reserved
Copyright © 2024 by Curtis Jones

No part of this publication may be reproduced, distributed, or transmitted in any form or by any means, including photocopying, recording, or other electronic or mechanical methods, without the prior written permission of the publisher, except in the case of brief quotations embodied in critical reviews and certain other noncommercial uses permitted by copyright law.

Published by Spines

ISBN: 979-8-89569-495-4

INTRODUCTION

This is not a story about a simple Bigfoot sighting. It is, instead, a completely true and unique story that involves an interaction I had with three mystical creatures called Yeti or Sasquatch, but most commonly known as Bigfoot. However, I will be referring to them as the "Shadow Men." This encounter had such a profound impact on me that it changed the way I looked at nature as I knew it. It took me 41 years to finally get around to telling my story in such detail. This was the first and last time I would ever experience anything as intense and terrifying as what I'm about to tell in my story.

My name is Chris Johanson, and I wasn't a believer in a lot of things growing up, especially monsters,

UFOs, and such. I was the type of person who couldn't be persuaded to believe in something simply by word of mouth alone. I believe in scientific evidence and, most of the time, what my eyes tell me. That's why I'm so skeptical about religion and the stories I've read from the Holy Bible. Those stories have been written and rewritten many times over thousands of years, and the stories usually get bigger and highly exaggerated over time. I'm not saying that religion doesn't have its place, but unfortunately, that place is not with me.

I was born Christopher Eaton in Northern California in 1968 along with my twin brother Rick, and when I was Five my mom divorced my father, then moved my siblings and I to Oregon, where she met and married my stepdad, Louie Johanson. I was nine at the time and he adopted us soon after. Now, we would be forever known as the Johanson family. When I was twelve, I asked to be called Chris because I felt that Christopher V Johanson was way too long to write out.

My mother, Shelly, never had a regular 9-to-5 job as far as I can remember. She was a stay-at-home mom who was happy collecting food stamps while my stepdad hit the daily grind, day after day. A couple of hundred-dollar welfare checks that came in the mail on the 3rd of every month were nice as well. My mom made an art form out of milking the system. "Why work when the government sends you free money?" I've heard my mom say to my stepdad many times.

My stepdad was a little rough around the edges and quite the disciplinarian, which came my way the majority of the time. However, he did provide for the family.

He was a baby boomer from Oklahoma and was a bit racist toward the Black community. When he was ten or so, he came to live in Oregon along with his nine siblings. Then, because of the lack of family income, he was forced to drop out of the seventh grade and found a job delivering newspapers.

We were a family that moved from town to town throughout the state, like "gypsies." As a result, my siblings and I attended over 50 different schools from kindergarten to the eighth grade. I can't even count how many towns we lived in, not to mention apartment complexes and trailer parks.

I've told this Bigfoot story a handful of times throughout my life, with mixed reviews; most were from family and close friends. I would hope that those who know me consider me an honest and trustworthy person with integrity. Nevertheless, I want to try to guide you, the reader, through my story with an open mind.

If you can put yourselves in my shoes, you might just feel some of the emotions that I felt during this event. And if you are one of the lucky ones who has witnessed a sighting as well, then I believe that you'll especially find this story interesting. But if you decide that this story is just a story, then I hope that you, at least, enjoy it for what it is.

This encounter is something that I truly experienced and is one that I would most definitely not have believed myself if I hadn't seen it with my own eyes; and even then, I still might have had a little doubt if it weren't for the fact that others were there to witness it for themselves.

There were six of us in total, but only four who had a visual on the three Shadow Men. However, it was I who interacted with them on a more intimate level. I will say that this is as real to me as the sky is blue.

I'll point out that life in the 1980s was very different to what it's like in the present day. Things as convenient as home computers were not accessible to most people, let alone laptops. Social media was nonexistent, such as Google, Facebook, Tik Tok, Dating sights etc. Even the comfort of cell phones didn't become available till the 90s. Considering those facts, teenagers had to find a way to entertain themselves and socialize by their own means.

MY STORY

I was 15 years old when my parents brought me, my twin brother Rick, and my younger sister Valerie, or Val for short, to Yreka, California. We came to stay with our Aunt Cathy while our parents traveled to other towns in search of work. Considering my stepdad's lack of education, the job pool was very limited. However, he had plenty of experience working as a short-order cook in family restaurants.

Yreka was a small historic gold mining town located in the foothills of the Klamath National Forest in Northern California, with a population of 3,500 and an elevation of 3,700 ft. The dense, forested mountains to the west of town stretched about 150 miles, all the way to the Pacific Ocean, with no towns in between. On a clear, sunny day, you could see the majestic, high, snowy peak of Mt. Shasta, due southeast approximately forty miles away. Yreka had the most amazing panoramic views I had ever seen.

We arrived in the summer of 1983, and it didn't take long to start making friends. It was easy for Rick and me because people were intrigued and curious about twins, and we were obliged to answer even the most obvious questions if it meant making friends.

One of the first people that we befriended was Daniel Campbell, who had become a short-lived boyfriend of my sister, Val, and was a couple of years older than Rick and me. Tall and skinny with short, sandy-blonde hair, Daniel was a bit of a loner who exhibited a strange and creepy personality. The one thing that I really liked about Daniel was listening to his tall tales. One that stood out the most was a story about him serving time in the army as a paratrooper and being captured as a prisoner of war by Cambodian soldiers while he parachuted over the enemy lines. Then, he was tortured for two weeks before finally killing three of his captors. That story sounded a whole lot like the movie "Rambo" to me, which had premiered in 1982, the year before we arrived in Yreka. I came to find out later that he was a big fan of war movies.

Daniel was also a self-proclaimed outdoor survivalist, with the necessary skills to hunt, fish, trap, build shelters, and start a fire with a bow drill. I could only laugh and take that with a great assault. Nevertheless, Rick and I started referring to him as "Daniel Boone," an early explorer and frontiersman from the eighteenth century. Daniel loved that nickname so much that I think he might have truly thought he was an actual reincarnation.

Now, Val, on the other hand, even though she was my sister, I really didn't like her much, probably because my parents didn't discipline her like they did with me and my brother. That would explain why, at the tender age of thirteen, Val was nothing more than a little tramp who loved any guy, young or old, that would show her some attention. Let's face it, most guys found her quite homely, with a bad disposition and negative vibes. In other words, she wasn't easy to look at. Her coke bottle glasses, anorexic frame, and long, stringy, thin hair didn't do her any favors either. Daniel and she complemented each other quite nicely, if you ask me.

Gus and Robert Withers were brothers with whom we also acquainted ourselves, and they were the last two people who were there to witness the unbelievable sighting. They just happened to be twins as well. However, unlike Rick and me, they were fraternal twins and didn't look anything alike. They didn't even look like brothers with how different they were. Both, in their own way, were charismatic and charming, with a great sense of humor.

Gus was 6' 1", skinny frame and weighed 195lbs. His hair was reddish blonde and cut to shoulder length. He was a bit more social than his brother and could be quite humorous at times. He loved goofing around and making harmless practical jokes. The most interesting thing that I found with Gus is his love for comics, obtaining an impressive collection, possessing over five hundred comic books. His favorite part of the collection was from the Marvel Comic series.

Robert was a little more reserved and softer spoken, but equally likable and pleasant company. At 6'0 he was one inch shorter than his brother and weighed 45 lbs more, at 240 lbs. His bleached blonde hair reached the middle of his back. He, like his brother, liked joking around but only when following Gus's lead. Robert was better academically than his brother, especially in studying history and geography. He loved reading books on the revolutionary and civil wars, as well on the history of the rise and fall of the Roman Empire.

Rick and I met the brothers while we were kicking a hacky sack around at the city park down the street from the apartment complex. Kicking a hacky sack was something at which we excelled. It helped draw people to us and served as a great icebreaker. We've made many friends in the same fashion.

I don't recall the exact day that led up to the encounter, but I believe it was near the end of July, and it was a blistering one hundred degrees plus. It was so hot we couldn't spend much time outside during the heat of the day. This was because my siblings and I, unfortunately, were not blessed with the dark pigment chromosome needed to keep us from looking like lobsters.

Yreka was experiencing a six-year drought, which explains why there were reports of animals of all kinds coming down from the mountains in search of food and water—animals such as whitetail deer, coyotes, foxes, and so on. But it also invited something else to wander down into town from the dense forest to the west. Something that I would be coming face to face with.

As I mentioned before, the temperature was too warm for us to be outside in the daylight hours, so we were confined to the apartment where my aunt resided until the sun went down sometime in the early evening.

The apartment complex was located next door to the south side of the elementary school. There was easy access to the school grounds from the complex because there was no fence to separate the two properties. However, a ten-foot-wide access road built for the school maintenance workers was all that separated the two properties. On the whole west side of the school grounds was a lush, green, and well-maintained soccer/baseball field with the baseball diamond being located just at the northwest corner. The school had only two fences, with one being an eight-foot chain link fence that spanned the entire west side perimeter, and a four-foot fence to the noth side connecting to the chain link and ending to the back of the schoolhouse.

It was about 3 p.m., and Daniel had just arrived to visit Val while Rick and I were kicking back on the couch watching some TV. I don't recall what we were watching. It doesn't really matter because we were only passing the time anyway and couldn't wait for the sun to start coming down in a couple of hours. Meanwhile, Aunt Cathy was in the kitchen preparing my favorite dinner: goulash. This was a dish that was almost like having "spaghetti and meatballs," but instead of using spaghetti pasta, it was made with elbow macaroni. The great thing was that it was inexpensive to make and was even better as leftovers the next day.

At 5:15 p.m., Aunt Cathy had dinner ready for us. She offered Daniel a plate, but he respectfully declined, while the rest of us sat down at the dinner table and devoured the goulash in short order, with plenty left over.

After the grazing was complete, Rick and I reclaimed our spots on the couch, where I quickly dozed off in a relaxing dream world. I assumed that Rick had done the same. I was abruptly awakened from a not-so-memorable dream by an annoying and aggressive knock at the front door, and right away, I knew who it was. We were expecting the brothers, Gus and Robert, to show up at any time. Aunt Cathy answered the door, and it was Gus who was standing there, with Robert just behind him. Both had goofy, dumbass grins on their faces. I forgot to mention just how humorous these two could be at times, especially Gus, and this would be one of those times when they both decided to be a pair of comedians. After a moment of just standing there like idiots, both lowered their heads, looking like little eight-year-old kids, while pretending to kick pebbles on the ground. Then Gus, with a high, soft-spoken voice, said, "Can Chris and Rick come out to play?" At that moment, everybody in the room just lost it, including my aunt. I must admit, that was very funny. After composing myself, I responded with, "Well played, dudes." Then Rick and I stepped outside to join the brothers.

After standing outside for about five minutes or so, engaging in some random chit-chat, one of the brothers suggested that we should play "guns." At this point, Rick and I looked at each other and began to chuckle. But looking back at the two of them, we could tell that they were not joking. We were fifteen, for Christ's sake, and too old for those kinds of games. However, Rick and I did feel bad for our reaction to that idea, so we reluctantly agreed that it was a good idea. But we all decided, instead, to call the game "Search and Destroy," better known as "hide and go seek."

There were only four of us; however, I came up with an idea to recruit Val and Daniel, so I did just that and went back into the apartment and shortly returned with both. I didn't have to twist their arms because they were more than happy to join us. This was great; now we had a more exciting game by having a three-on-three battle royal. However, what no one realized was that I had a more devious and cunning plan in mind. I felt that this game was specifically tailored just for me.

So, here was my plan in a nutshell: placing the two lovebirds, Val and Daniel, on my team so that I could use them later as my sacrificial lambs for the other team to come in for the kill. Then I would swoop in to slaughter the other team all at once. I know it sounds diabolical; however, the game wouldn't have been as fun without throwing a little twist in the mix. This is what I call "Game On!"

Now that the teams had been established, it was time to get on the move. We all voted, and Daniel was chosen to toss a coin to see which team would be departing first. As team captains, it was between Rick and me, but I let Rick choose the toss. As Daniel tossed a quarter five feet in the air, Rick called out, "Heads." Unfortunately, it was bad luck for him because it landed tails up. Then I chose my team to be the first out of the gate, while Ricks team remained and had to count down from 100 to give my team ample time to create some distance between us.

Prior to the coin toss, we came up with a simple rule for the game. We were confined to stay within the school grounds and no more than twenty feet beyond the eight-foot chain-link fence on the west side of the grounds.

It was about 6:30, and the sun was just heading over the mountains to the west, leaving us with at least a hundred feet of visibility and enough darkness to allow my team to remain undetected by the other team upon completing their countdown.

Once the countdown commenced, my team and I bolted off in a full-out sprint as I led the pack, with Val and Daniel right on my tail. I already knew beforehand the location where I wanted to position us. The spot I chose was behind the baseball diamond at the northeast corner of the school grounds.

Instead of traveling on a straight path through the soccer field to that location, we needed to take a not-so-obvious route, so we headed north, around the east side of the school, then turned west along the outer edge of the border, making it to our location—hopefully undetected. However, Val slowed us down a bit because she was running out of steam due to our initial takeoff. It took about five minutes, but I was okay with that.

Once we got to the corner of the school grounds, we hopped over the four-foot metal fence and quickly took to the ground on our bellies, right behind the baseball diamond, as planned.

Facing the back of the baseball diamond, I was lying down on the left, while Val was just to my right and Daniel was to the right side of her. Behind us stood the eight-foot chain-link fence, connected to the four-foot fence at the corner and spanning all the way down the west side perimeter of the school grounds, then ending where the apartment complex and school property line met. Also behind us was an unlocked man gate attached to the chain-link fence, a couple of feet from the corner, which allowed us access for an unexpected getaway if need be.

Behind the fence line lay a large area of undeveloped land spanning west, a quarter of a mile, and it was covered with two feet of tall grass and even taller weeds. Additionally, four-foot dirt mounds covered in dry grass were scattered throughout the landscape, as well as an occasional thorn bush. The only trees that could be seen were visible far off in the distance, where you could also see four or five homes that were illuminated with lights. Beyond that was where the dense, woody forest began.

Now that I have laid out the topographical area in

fair detail, this will be the part of the story where it begins to get mysterious, exciting, and scary at the same time for me.

It's been ten minutes or so since arriving at our location, and I haven't seen or heard a single soul as I scan my eyes back and forth intently within the school grounds. While focusing on the task at hand, Val and Daniel had other things on their minds: each other. They were more interested in playing "touchy-feely," which I found both annoying and sickening at the same time. I did try to tune them out; however, that didn't last long, so I put a stop to it by letting them know that I needed their help focusing on the game. But that was easier said than done.

It was about 6:55, and the sun had fallen well over the mountains at this point, exposing the millions of bright stars in the sky, which provided us with enough light to see the silhouettes of both the schoolhouse and the apartments diagonally across the soccer field from us. The streetlights on the other side of the buildings provided us with extra lighting as well.

We waited patiently and eagerly for the enemy to finally show itself because I knew that they would be the ones to make the first move and come looking. We were intent on letting the fight come to us, which gave my team the advantage over my brothers' team.

As I was lying there in a comfortable and relaxed state, I dozed off, which left us in a vulnerable position, only because I had no trust in my teammates to successfully stand a proper watch. They both made it clear, through their actions, that they really had no interest in playing this game from the get-go. I don't know how long I was out for, but I was too comfortable to care.

My eyes suddenly opened when Val poked me in the ribs to let me know that both she and Daniel might have a possible visual on Rick and his team. I had to rub my eyes to clear the haze so I could get a good sight of the assumed enemy for myself. Once my eyes were clear, I focused in on the subjects in question and determined that there was, in fact three figures walking from the south side of the schoolhouse heading towards the soccer field and about to pass in front of us, approximately sixty yards away, and due to the lack of good lighting, we were only able to make out their silhouettes.

At this point in my story, you've probably already guessed that what we were looking at was not Rick, Gus, or Robert, but, in fact, it was the Shadow Men that

I mentioned at the beginning—Bigfoot, to be exact. However, at this moment, my teammates and I were still fully unaware of what we were witnessing. If I had recognized them for what they really were, then that would have been the end of my story. The real story is just about to begin.

While the Shadow Men made their way to the center of the soccer field, a hundred feet from my team's position behind the baseball diamond, my idiotic teammate, Daniel, was preparing to rush in for a surprise ambush. But I had to quickly talk him down and explain to him that we were too far away to make a move like that. Instead, I came up with the idea to make our way to the other side of the chain-link fence, where we could have a better chance of having the element of surprise. He agreed with that plan; then I turned to face the gate and proceeded to crawl toward it with Daniel and Val in tow. When I got to the gate, and before moving forward, I turned my head to see the three "Shadow" men heading over the fence, one after another, about a hundred feet down the line.

We got ourselves to the other side, then I led my team, at a snail's pace, in the direction where I saw the Shadow men cross over. After getting fifty yards down the fence line, we decided to stop and make this the spot to hunker down and wait. I was hoping that the other team would move in our direction so that we would have the advantage of spotting them before they spotted us. But I wouldn't have known that maybe my brother wouldn't be around because they just might have seen something in the darkness themselves that could've scared them away. Nevertheless, as I rested there with my back against the fence, looking in all directions, it seemed that we were alone with nothing but the sound of crickets. In other words, it looked as if both my team and my brother's team were at a stalemate, and neither one of us wanted to advance on the other.

Even though we had just settled in our spot for a minute or two, Val and Daniel were getting a bit restless and quite flirtatious with one another. So, I was more than relieved when my sister informed me that they were going to crawl out into the tall weeds so that they could best aid me if I happened to come under attack. But I didn't buy that from the second it came out of her mouth. Nevertheless, knowing my sister the way that I do and observing their actions, I knew what their true intentions were. I really didn't care anyway, because all I wanted at that point was for them to get the hell away from me. So, I just bid them farewell and said, "Have fun," to both as they slithered away like a pair of snakes in the grass. I didn't pay any attention to which direction they headed off to because I was too focused on scanning my eyes around in search of the enemy.

After staring down the fence line for a moment, I leaned back against the fence with my head facing forward and closed my eyes for a minute. I reopened my eyes when I heard my teammates giggling like little schoolgirls, and as I looked out into the tall weeds, I noticed two figures sitting or squatting on top of a grassy dirt mound, slightly to my left, about twenty feet in front of me.

Remember, at this point, I was still fully unaware of what was sitting there looking back at me with curiosity and wonder. As far as I was concerned, it was just Val and Daniel sitting there, relaxed and without a care in the world. Although I did find it odd that they were exposing themselves to be easily picked off by the enemy, the only reason it didn't draw any attention from me at the time was that they were just calmly sitting there with no worries. Meanwhile, Val and Daniel were lying somewhere in the tall weeds just a few feet away, with no clue about what was going on. The funny thing was that they were even closer to the Shadow Men than I was.

What's about to happen in the next series of events is going to change everything that I've ever known or even thought I knew, especially because I've always considered myself someone who has a logical mind and some basic common sense. However, on this night, all of that would be put to the ultimate test.

There I was, sitting there with my back against the fence, continually rotating my head from left to right, slowly, hoping that I would get some sign of the other team, even though I only had about twenty-five feet of visibility to work with. Every time my head moved back to the left from the right, my eyes would take a quick glance at the two sitting on the mound of dirt, and nothing in their demeanor changed. They just sat there, staring at me intently and motionless.

What felt, to me, like a long period of time—just sitting there with nothing but my thoughts—was only about four minutes from the time that we first arrived at that spot. However, time was irrelevant to me because I was totally content with just sitting there, and it wouldn't bother me a bit if I fell asleep and didn't wake until the morning.

I was making another rotation with my head, as I had been doing for the last few minutes; however, this time it was different. As my head was turning again from the right to the left, and just as my eyes were in line with the Shadow Men on the dirt mound, I was completely startled when I saw a shadowy figure come racing out of the darkness just behind and to the left of the two sitting on the mound. As this figure was making its way around the backside of the mound, the other two stood up rapidly and with some urgency. At that moment, I realized that the two who had been sitting there the whole time, watching me, were not my teammates at all. Instead, in my own mind, I was looking at the other team finally coming in for the kill. Little did I know how wrong I would be.

After making its way around the other two, the figure who had just arrived from out of the dark had its eyes fixed on me and was heading in my direction with considerable speed. Suddenly, I felt a dose of adrenaline rush throughout my body as my heartbeat elevated intensely. Then, before the Shadow Man could get much closer, I was able to get to my feet, raise my right arm, take aim with my imaginary pistol, and began blasting away as I yelled, "Bang! Bang! Bang!" at the top of my lungs. It suddenly stopped just ten feet away.

At this moment, my gut was telling me that something was just not right with this picture. This human-like figure appeared to be a tad bit larger than anyone on my brother's team would've been; however, I just attributed it to the darkness. I couldn't get a view of the Shadow Man's face, but I did notice something odd. It looked as if it were wearing a thick fur coat when, in fact, it was hair that covered its body from the head down to its feet.

Then, just as quickly as it had stopped, all three of the Shadow men turned and began running and leaping through the tall weeds and toward the houses off in the distance. With a combination of the stars in the sky and well-lit houses in the background, I could see all three of them as they twisted their upper bodies every few steps, just to look back at me, as if to make sure I wasn't following.

Once I saw them begin to leap while taking unusually large strides, I must've gone into a deep state of shock because when I began to yell again, the only words that would come out of my mouth were "Deer!" repeatedly. Even though I could see that what I was clearly looking at was traveling on two feet, it was probably due to their leaping so high through the weeds that sent me into shock.

After I stopped shouting and my mind began to come back into focus, I noticed both Val and Daniel were standing next to me. I'm assuming that they had jumped up from out of the tall weeds where they were frolicking about when they heard all the commotion going on. It was unfortunate for them that they didn't get the chance or the privilege to witness the Shadow Men as I did. Even though, it did frighten the hell out of me. The only thing that they could see at this point, was three shadowy figures in the distance running towards the hills. All that we could do now was watch, while they get further away as they fade into the darkness.

I was still a bit in shock, trying to process in my mind everything that had just occurred. The thought of the Shadow Men being a Bigfoot family didn't even register in my brain. The easiest way for me to explain it was that, while my eyes were telling me one thing, my brain was telling me something different.

I heard my brother's voice from somewhere behind me, off in the distance, yelling out my name, "Chris!" repeatedly. He and the brothers were running in my direction from the south side of the schoolhouse, crossing the soccer field. I turned and walked back to the chain-link fence, locking my fingers between the intertwining links with both hands. Then, when Rick got within twenty feet of me, he yelled out, "Hey, we saw Bigfoot!" Once I heard those words come out of his mouth, I instantly felt a fear that I had never experienced before in my life. Suddenly, all the blood rushed out of my head, and everything just went blank. The next memory that I had was of me on the other side of the chain-link fence, running as fast as my feet could go toward the center of the soccer field, where I finally stopped and fell to my knees while putting my hands over my eyes and face as tears began running down my cheeks. It's hard to explain all the thoughts and emotions that I was feeling throughout my body. My head was so scrambled with thoughts that I didn't even notice that everyone else in the group was standing over me. I was just kneeling there, still in shock, shaking and shivering as if it was thirty degrees outside, even though it was a warm ninety-five.

Finally, I was slowly coming out of my shock and could hear my brother and the others speaking to me, even though I didn't understand a word that anybody was saying. Nevertheless, I did feel some comfort knowing that I was out of reach from those monstrous, hairy beasts that could've torn me apart at any time, especially knowing how close the third Shadow Man came to me. But, in all actuality, the Shadow Men had not shown one ounce of aggression toward me at any time.

After thirty minutes or so, I was feeling about ninety percent back to normal and could comprehend what everyone was saying; however, I was still a bit shaken over the ordeal. Even though I felt safe, I found myself constantly looking over at the chain-link fence, just in case something might still be out there.

We were still standing in midfield and decided to sit down in a tight circle, facing each other, so that we could share notes. That way, we could paint a bigger picture of what had transpired between each of us. I chose to sit facing the chain-link fence only because I didn't feel completely convinced that we were alone.

Now that we have sat down in a cozy, compact circle, Rick, Gus, Robert, Daniel, and Val all had their eyes glued on me. They wanted to hear from me first because I had the most direct contact with the Shadow Men, not to mention, emotionally traumatized by the ordeal.

As I told the story from my viewpoint, everyone was completely fixated on every word that rolled out of my mouth. Then, when I came to the part of the story where Rick had informed me that his team saw Bigfoot, I started to get a little anxious and began shivering again, as if I were back in that moment. We put the discussion on pause so that I could regain my composure.

A couple of minutes later, we continued our discussion, but now I was interested in what everyone else had to share from their viewpoint. However, there were two who really didn't have anything to add. That would be Val and Daniel, who were playing "grab ass" the majority of the time with each other in the tall weeds. Nevertheless, that didn't keep Daniel from trying, as he began to tell some half-witted story. However, Val had to stop him before he could make a complete ass out of himself. The fact is, Daniel just didn't want to feel left out and was probably a bit jealous of me for having the privilege of witnessing something that most people would find exciting and adventurous. I must admit, I did feel honored and privileged to experience something that unique, even if it did scare the living hell out of me.

Now, Rick's story may not have been as compelling as mine, but it was just as important because it was the confirmation that I needed so that I could fit all the pieces of the puzzle together in my head and make sense of it all. However, the only thing that didn't make any sense to me was the reason why these mythical creatures would be roaming around in a rural town like Yreka.

All Rick could tell me was that he and the brothers were lying down on their bellies, right on the property line of the school grounds and apartment complex, as they witnessed the three figures walking toward the chain-link fence, while my team was on the opposite side of the school grounds, behind the baseball diamond, unaware of what Rick's team was looking at. But the difference between their sighting and ours was that the three figures were about fifty feet from them, and they had some better lighting, which allowed the team a better view of the creatures. At that moment, when they became aware that what they were looking at was a family of three Bigfoot, they immediately retreated to the safety of the apartment complex. This is where they remained until, minutes later, they could hear my yells.

It all began to make sense now, after collaborating with the other team, so I felt confident that what I had encountered was a family of Bigfoot. Nevertheless, before I can say for certain, I need to examine whatever evidence I have at my disposal. All that I have is some circumstantial evidence to go on, which I find very compelling. I'm going to look at the known facts so I can paint a picture and explain why I'm positively sure of what I and the others have witnessed.

First, let's look back into the story, where my team is lying down behind the baseball diamond, where we see what we thought was my brother's team. Even if my team was unable to make a positive identification of the Shadow Men, it was Rick, Gus, and Robert who were able to clearly confirm that they, without a shadow of a doubt, were looking at a family of Bigfoot. And since I had my own individual encounter with the creatures, I had no reason whatsoever to disbelieve them. So, when I look back and evaluate all that I have experienced, it ties everything together.

For me, it started when I was sitting down with my back against the chain-link fence, with two of them just staring at me from the moment I noticed them, and they remained completely silent and motionless the whole time. Then, when the third creature came out of the darkness and stopped momentarily within ten feet of where I was standing, I could see that it was covered with fur or hair from head to toe. But the most compelling part of this scenario was the fact that I yelled out the word "Deer" repeatedly. This action alone confirms that I was witnessing something that didn't even remotely look or feel like anything other than the legendary mystical creature known as Bigfoot. On that note, there wouldn't have been any reason for me to yell out the word "Deer," especially if they had been recognizable figures.

All that I can say now is that when you combine my experience with Rick, Gus, and Robert's accounts, there are just too many coincidences for me to simply dismiss the idea that "Bigfoot" is somewhere out there.

The following morning, my brother and I were up early at about 6:30 a.m., and the only thing we wanted to talk about was the encounter. Since we were the only ones awake in the apartment, we had to use our whisper voices. But it was hard to do, considering the subject of our discussion. As we were in the middle of eating our bowl of Wheaties for breakfast, Rick came up with a great plan for the day. The plan was set; we were heading to the library, which opened at 11:00 a.m. That was going to be another four hours. So, we finished our Wheaties, plopped ourselves on the couch, and began watching our favorite program, "Scooby-Doo." Yes, even at 15, we loved our cartoons.

At 8:45, cartoon hour was over as Daniel came

knocking. I was the lucky one to be sitting closest to the door, so I got up and answered it. Right off the bat, he wanted us to follow him to the school ground because he had something urgent to show us. Not a "Good morning" or "Hey dudes," nothing. Of course, we followed him. Val was still sleeping, and Daniel wasn't interested in her. So, we didn't bother waking her. I think the honeymoon was over between the two of them anyway.

He didn't want to tell us what it was until we got there, keeping us in suspense. We just followed him in a slow jog. It only took all of thirty seconds, and we were at the spot where he made a big discovery.

We were in the children's playground, just behind the schoolhouse, standing next to the swing set. Daniel then pointed down to the hard, pebbly dirt to reveal to Rick and me what looked like three large footprints. However, upon further inspection, they just didn't look right to me. Even at age 15, my brother and I were not bamboozled by his antics. It was clear that these prints were scratched in with a stick or something like it, then made with hands to create indentations in the ground. It was obvious that Daniel was desperately making a last-ditch effort to contribute his part to the story, especially after his last attempt failed. But since Rick and I didn't want to make him feel bad, we just shrugged it off and quickly presented our plan to go to the library so we could do some research on Bigfoot. Daniel was all for that. I figured that even he couldn't screw that up, right?

We were fortunate that the library was only a couple of blocks up the street from the school, and since all of us possessed a library card, it was a no-brainer to spend our day in a controlled atmosphere. We were already taking a big chance being outside while the sun got higher in the sky.

We got to the library and still had about an hour and a half until the doors opened, so we found a nice, shady pine tree to stand under while we waited.

As soon as the doors opened, we immediately found the book index, located next to the desk where the librarian usually hung out. All three of us were in search of anything "Bigfoot." I was specifically looking for nonfiction because I wanted to read eyewitness accounts from real people with ordinary lives. I found tons of books and magazines as well. I just couldn't possibly read all of them. But Rick and Daniel were there as well, and there was plenty of reading material for each of us.

I found so many stories that echoed my own experience that I had with these elusive creatures. Then I got
some help from a little eighty something year old
librarian sitting behind the desk. I didn't know she was
even there until I heard a soft cough coming from
behind the four-foot desk, where she sat in a chair on
wheels. She was probably no taller than five-feet tall, if
she were standing, that is. Anyway, the sweat little old
lady helped me locate a bundle of historic newspaper
articles from the Yreka Gazette dating back to the early
1900s, finding many reported claims of Bigfoot sightings
near the town of Yreka, however, no reported sighting in
the town itself.

Daniel, Rick, and I were finally booted out of the
library at 5:00 p.m., at closing time. I just couldn't
believe that we spent that much time cramming all that
information into our tiny little minds. Daniel was a
good reader and seemed to comprehend the material
just fine. Rick and I, on the other hand, had a general
comprehension, but we had always been below-average
readers growing up. So, we could only absorb so much.
Nevertheless, Rick and I did gain a great deal of insight.

Now that we've done all that research and learned
so much about Bigfoot, what would we do with all that

knowledge? The answer to that question would be, "Absolutely nothing." Who would we tell? Or better yet, what would we say? "Well, officer, last evening we saw three hairy monsters at the grade school, playing on the swing set." I don't think so. All three of us decided to do what made the most sense to us. Instead of opening ourselves up to public humiliation and embarrassment, we would just keep our story locked up in our heads and let it fade away into a distant memory.

Daniel faded into our memory as well because he had moved out of town shortly after the encounter. But I can imagine that he has told his version of the story many times to whoever would listen. The story probably grew bigger and more strange every time he told it.

The night of the encounter was the last time Rick and I hung out with Gus and Robert, even though we saw them pretty much every day while attending high school that year. After all, we had only known them for about a week or so before that night, which would only make them acquaintances, anyway.

We never tried telling Aunt Cathy what had happened that night, but she did catch wind of it some years later through our parents, who didn't believe a word of it. They did think it was a great bedtime story that I could tell my children someday.

It didn't matter if both Rick and I had witnessed this Bigfoot family at the same time, from different vantage points or not. No matter how adamant we were while telling our account, we got pretty much the same reactions. However, that would change when I was thirty-three, working on a ship as a merchant mariner.

Jason Sutton was the 1st Mate aboard the same ship that I worked on, and we had become close friends. One day, Jason and I were sitting in the galley eating some lunch while the rest of the crew was either out on the back deck or in their staterooms snoozing. Then, out of the blue, Jason looked straight at me and said, "So, tell me about Bigfoot." At that moment, I got a bit embarrassed only because I thought that my captain, with his big mouth, had repeated the story back to him and now wanted to make fun of me. But that wasn't the case. It turns out that Jason likes to ask that question to everyone he meets and asks it just as bluntly as he did to me. He does that to make sure that he can get a sincere and honest reaction.

Once he saw me react the way that I had, he was intent on getting that story out of me. So, I gave it to him. He knew that the story was very real because he could see the emotions I had as I was telling it. I even started to shake a little when I came to the part of the story where I went into an incapacitated state of shock. Jason was already a believer in Bigfoot from hearing other testimonies; however, after listening to mine, he became even more of a believer. More than that, we became closer as friends that lasts even today.

FINAL THOUGHTS

I'm no closer now than I was forty-one years ago to finding out exactly what it was that I, and the others in my party, encountered that night back in 1983. However, with all the circumstantial evidence, and with what I had seen with my own eyes, it was something human-like, yet not human at all. Therefore, the only logical conclusion that I can come up with is that this could have only been a family of "Bigfoot."

The fact that these elusive mystical creatures have been able to navigate throughout our national forests without capture is beyond my comprehension. Another thing to take note of is that, with the thousands of reported sightings over the years, it doesn't make any sense to me that all would be witnessing a hoax or creating one themselves. Nevertheless, there's no shortage of those who have tried. Whenever I come across reports, I do the best that I can to weed out the stories that sound likely from the unlikely. In my opinion, I sincerely hope that Bigfoot remains hidden deep in the forests because history has shown that man can be cruel. Taking them out of their natural habitat would be a tragic injustice to their species. Telling the stories of them coming out from the shadows only helps keep their legend alive.

I will close with my favorite quote of all time: "When the legend becomes fact, print the legend."

9 7 9 8 8 8 9 5 6 9 4 9 5 4